150 ROUNDS
For Singing and Teaching

Edward Bolkovac and Judith Johnson

BOOSEY & HAWKES

This collection is dedicated to all teachers who enjoy sharing
the gift of music with children.

Special thanks to Des, Éva, Karl and Anthony for their understanding. A very special thanks to Anne Comiskey and Karen Girard without whose devotion, hard work and patience the timely completion of this collection would not have been possible. Additional thanks to Peggy, Tacey, Jerie, Danny and Ruth, Kathryn, Patrick, and Toni for help with texts, translations and computer work.

Ah, Poor Bird*

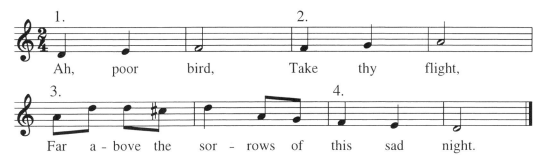

Ah, poor bird, Take thy flight,
Far a-bove the sor-rows of this sad night.

The source of this modern English text is unknown. The music seems to be based on the minor key version of *Oh, My Love* found in *The Catch Club, 1762*. This round can be sung as part of a quodlibet with *Rose, Rose* and/or *Hey, Ho, Nobody Home*.

Alleluia

18th Century

Al – le – lu – ia, Al – le – lu – ia,
Al – le – lu – ia, Al – le – lu – ia.

Alleluia*

Israeli

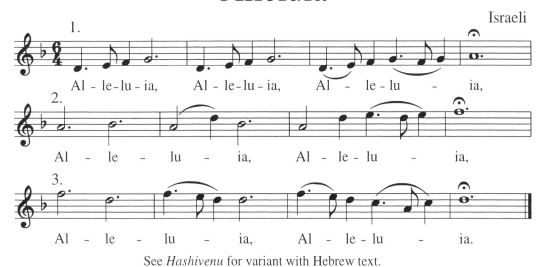

Al – le-lu – ia, Al – le-lu – ia, Al – le-lu – ia,
Al – le – lu – ia, Al – le – lu – ia,
Al – le – lu – ia, Al – le – lu – ia.

See *Hashivenu* for variant with Hebrew text.

A Boat

John Jenkins (1592-1687)
The Musical Companion, 1673

A boat, a boat! Haste to the fer-ry!

For we'll go o - ver to be mer - ry!

To laugh ___ and ___ sing and drink old sher-ry!

Adiuva Nos, Deus*

Pammelia, 1609

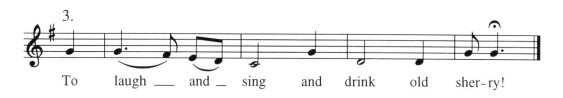

A - diu - va nos, De -

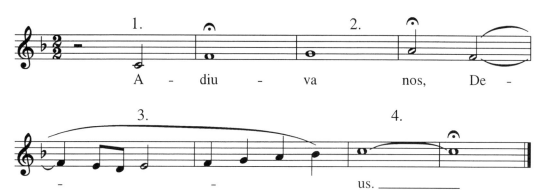

- us. ___

Translation: Help us, God.

PERFORMING THE ROUNDS

1. Starting: The numbers above the staves indicate the number of parts needed to sing the round. The position of these numbers indicates **when** each group must start singing the round from the beginning. Before singing in parts, the choir may sing the entire piece together in unison.

2. Ending: There are two ways to end rounds:

    a) Separately: Each group sings the entire round a predetermined number of times. The group that enters first, will finish first. The last group to enter will be the last to sing.

    b) Together: Rounds that have a clear harmonic cadence may sound well when ended together on a chord. The singers must be made aware of the fact that after a certain number of repetitions, the director or song leader will end the piece at any one of the optional fermatas. A simple signal from the conductor indicates that the singers are to stop at the upcoming fermata and hold the note till the conductor gives a final cut-off. Even though the singers may be in the middle of a word or phrase, the over-all effect of such a harmonic cadence can be quite satisfying. Since most of the fermatas are only suggestions, other points of cadence may be chosen that are equally convincing.

3. Performance Suggestions: Any choral program, certain plays, madrigal dinners and social events can be enriched by the inclusion of a group of rounds. When performing rounds the choir may stand together in a regular choral formation or the different groups may be physically separated to utilize the acoustical properties of the performance space. If the singers are very confident, they may even stand around or among the members of the audience for a unique sound experience. To encourage active participation, the audience may be asked to sing one of the parts with the help of a few well-placed singers. Although a cappella is the preferred method of singing these rounds, discreet accompaniments may be occasionally devised for finger cymbals, drums and other percussion instruments for an added rhythmic effect. Occasionally, tasteful instrumental doublings may provide an extra opportunity for a few talented students. Some pieces are marked as suitable for a quodlibet, one or more harmonically compatible rounds which can be sung together.

4. Formatting: Many of the rounds on pages 1-59 are typeset in a basic wrap-around format in which individual lines are not aligned. Students singing from these scores benefit aurally because they cannot simultaneously see the other parts, and must listen keenly in the manner of orchestral players. Many of the rounds with texts are presented again in choral score format on pages 64-84. Here, the various parts are lined up exactly, facilitating harmonic analysis and providing easy, readable scores for conductors. Rounds that are also presented in score format are marked with an asterisk after the title.

EDITORIAL CONSIDERATIONS

The rounds are numbered and presented in alphabetical order by title. Musical and textual sources are acknowledged immediately above each piece: textual sources are on the left; musical sources are on the right. Since most of the rounds included in this collection have taken shape over the course of many centuries and been transformed and adapted by many different cultures, deciding on a definitive original source seems presumptuous. Consequently, a musical source is included only when a round is attributed to a specific composer or when a piece was found by the editors in an 'early' collection (mid-19th century or earlier). Most of the rounds included with no musical sources have no conclusive origin, but can easily be found in countless modern collections and music series books. The editors would greatly appreciate any additional source or composer information verifiable from other 'early' collections or any corrections in general for possible inclusion in future printings.

Some rounds fall clearly into a given time signature, while others may be transcribed in more than one way depending on their interpretation. Certain pieces can withstand greater tempo and agogic flexibility than others. In this collection, an attempt was made to choose time signatures based on the agogic integrity of the texts and the musical character of each round. Teachers and conductors will have to decide for themselves which time signatures are best suited. **Let the musical character be the deciding factor, not pedagogical or conductorial convenience!**

Key signatures were chosen for elementary school children with mid-range voices. The rounds may be transposed, however, to best suit the vocal ability and range of each particular class or choir.

Fermatas are used to indicate a place where the singers may end together on a cadence. Although some of the 'early' sources include fermatas, **most fermata signs in this collection are editorial suggestions only.** Some rounds were transcribed without fermatas, however, because of their smaller dimensions or lack of convincing cadence points. Most rounds transcribed with fermatas may also be ended separately or other potential cadence points may be discovered. The decision to end a round separately or together or to add or change the place of fermatas must be based on the individual musical character of each piece.

TABLE OF CONTENTS

All into Service*

Pammelia, 1609

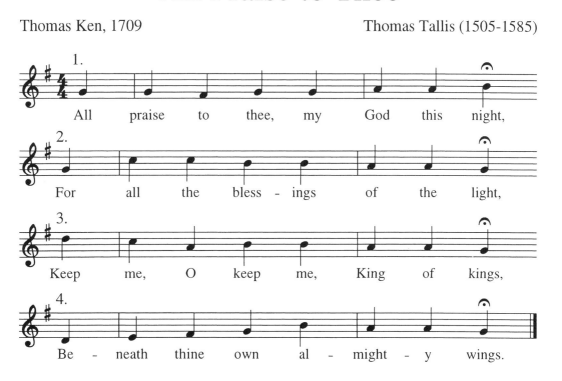

All in - to ser - vice,

Let us sing mer - ri - ly to - geth -

er: Ding, dong, ding, dong bell.

All Praise to Thee

Thomas Ken, 1709   Thomas Tallis (1505-1585)

All praise to thee, my God this night,

For all the bless - ings of the light,

Keep me, O keep me, King of kings,

Be - neath thine own al - might - y wings.

All Things Shall Perish

German

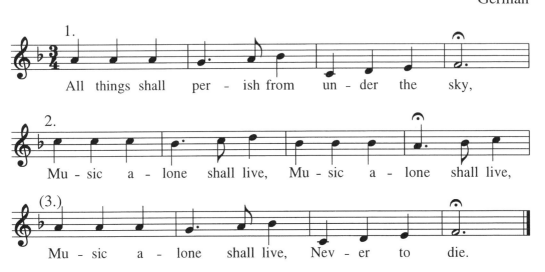

All things shall per - ish from un - der the sky,

Mu - sic a - lone shall live, Mu - sic a - lone shall live,

Mu - sic a - lone shall live, Nev - er to die.

These English words are based on the original anonymous German text. This round can also be sung in three parts as part of a quodlibet with *Coffee* and/or *With Laughter and Singing*.

A Ram Sam Sam*

Moroccan

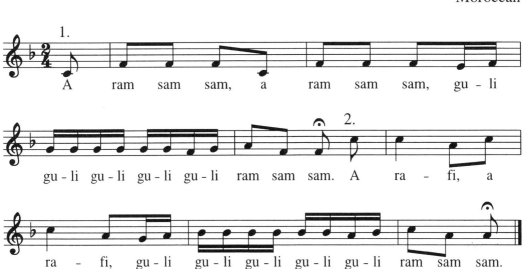

A ram sam sam, a ram sam sam, gu - li

gu - li gu - li gu - li gu - li ram sam sam. A ra - fi, a

ra - fi, gu - li gu - li gu - li gu - li gu - li ram sam sam.

This text is composed of nonsense syllables.

Are You Sleeping?

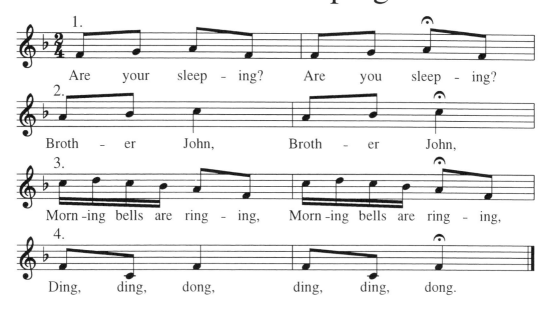

1. Are your sleep - ing? Are you sleep - ing?
2. Broth - er John, Broth - er John,
3. Morn -ing bells are ring - ing, Morn -ing bells are ring - ing,
4. Ding, ding, dong, ding, ding, dong.

French text:

Frère Jacques, Frère Jacques,
Dormez vous? dormez vous?
Sonnez les matines, sonnez les matines,
Din, don, din, din, don, din.

Spanish text:

Fray Felipe, Fray Felipe,
¿Duer-mes tú? ¿Duer-mes tú?
Toca la campana, toca la campana,
Tin-tín, tan, tin-tín, tan.

At Summer Morn*

The School Round Book, 1852

1. At sum - mer morn _ the mer - ry lark her - alds
in the day, 2. At e - ven - tide sad Phil - lo -
mel breathes _ her plain - tive lay, 3. Warb -
ling sweet - ly all __ her grief _ a - way.

Philomel is a figure from classical mythology who was turned into a nightingale.

TXB-86

Beaux Yeux*

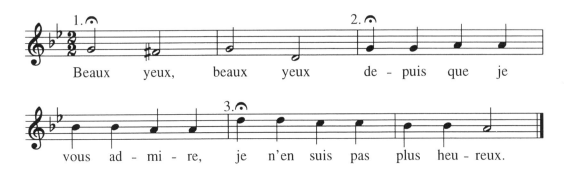

Beaux yeux, beaux yeux de - puis que je

vous ad - mi - re, je n'en suis pas plus heu - reux.

Translation: Lovely eyes, since I have been admiring you, I am no longer happy.
French variant of *Rose, Rose.*

The Bell Doth Toll*

The Vocal Companion, 1810–1812

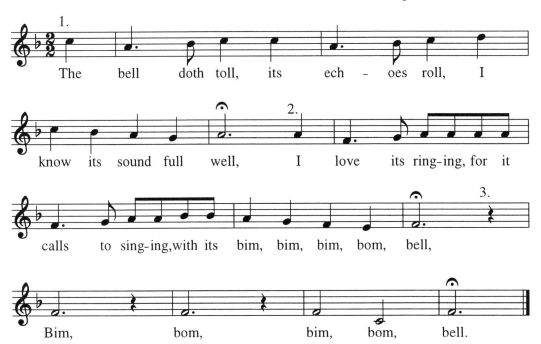

The bell doth toll, its ech - oes roll, I

know its sound full well, I love its ring-ing, for it

calls to sing-ing, with its bim, bim, bim, bom, bell,

Bim, bom, bim, bom, bell.

Alternate text: Sing to the Lord, Sing to the Lord a joyful song of praise. *(2 times.)*
Praise, praise, praise the Lord.

The Birch Tree*

Russian

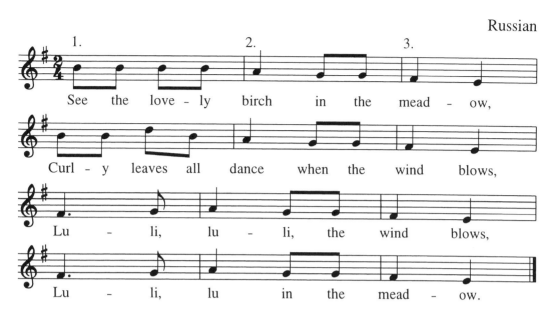

See the love - ly birch in the mead - ow,

Curl - y leaves all dance when the wind blows,

Lu - li, lu - li, the wind blows,

Lu - li, lu in the mead - ow.

This Russian folk melody is used in the fourth movement, *Allegro con fuoco,* of Tchaikovsky's Symphony No. 4 in F minor.

Brother Martin

Broth - er Mar - tin, Broth - er Mar - tin,

wake, a - wake, wake, a - wake, The

bells ___ are ring - ing, the bells ___ are ring - ing,

Ding, dong, ding, ding dong, ding.

A minor key variant of *Are You Sleeping?*

This melody is used in the third movement, *Feierlich und gemessen, ohne zu schleppen,* of Mahler's Symphony No. 1 in D major.

Chairs to Mend*

William Hayes (1706–1777)

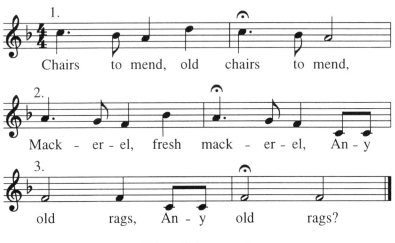

Chairs to mend, old chairs to mend,

Mack - er - el, fresh mack - er - el, An - y

old rags, An - y old rags?

Old English street cries

Cherries So Ripe*

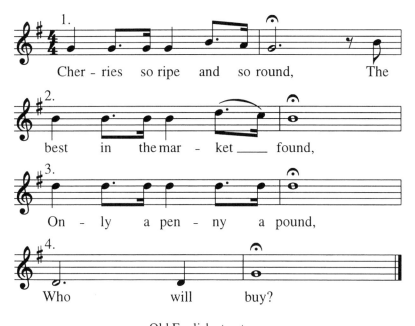

Cher - ries so ripe and so round, The

best in the mar - ket _____ found,

On - ly a pen - ny a pound,

Who will buy?

Old English street cry

Christmas is Coming

Several versions of this round use the word 'Christus' in place of 'Christmas'.

Coffee*

Elinor O'Connor   Karl Gottlieb Hering (1766–1853)

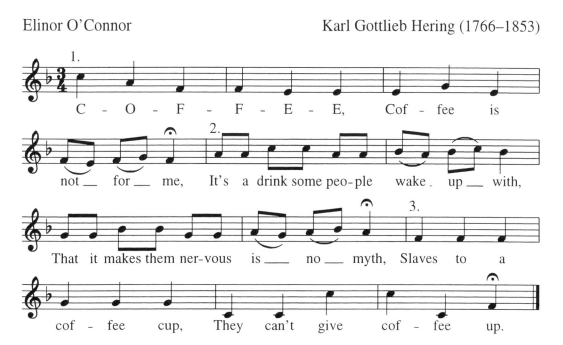

The author of the original German text is unknown. This round can be sung as part of a quodlibet with *All Things Shall Perish* and/or *With Laughter and Singing*.

Come Follow*

John Hilton (1599–1657)

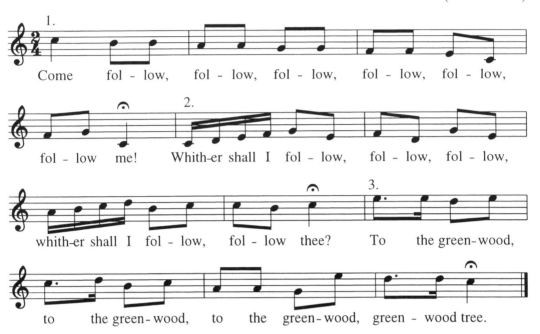

Come fol - low, fol - low, fol - low, fol - low, fol - low, fol - low me! Whith-er shall I fol - low, fol - low, fol - low, whith-er shall I fol - low, fol - low thee? To the green-wood, to the green-wood, to the green-wood, green - wood tree.

There are many variations of this round in a number of primary and secondary sources.

Come, Let's Be Singing

M. V. Exner

Israeli

Come, let's be sing - ing, Who'll then be - gin the song?
Come, let's be sing - ing, Who'll then be - gin the song?
Come, let's be sing - ing, Who'll then be - gin the - song?

See *Hava Nashira* for Hebrew text.

TXB-86

Come, Let's Dance

French, 13th Century

Come, let's dance and sing a song to-geth - er,

Come, we'll laugh and have a jol - ly time.

Conditur Kirie

Pammelia, 1609

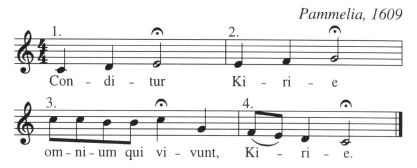

Con - di - tur Ki - ri - e

om - ni - um qui vi - vunt, Ki - ri - e.

Translation: Lord, Founder of everything that lives.

The Cuckoo

E. Bolkovac

Jacopo Gotfredo Ferrari (1759–1842)

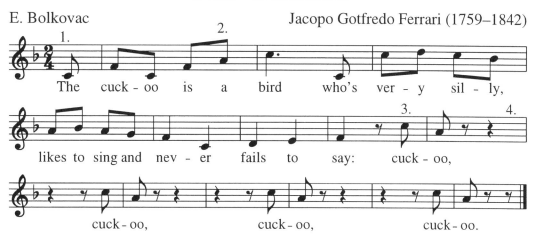

The cuck - oo is a bird who's ver - y sil - ly,

likes to sing and nev - er fails to say: cuck - oo,

cuck - oo, cuck - oo, cuck - oo.

Dame, Lend Me a Loaf*

Pammelia, 1609

Da Pacem, Domine*

Melchior Franck (1573–1639)

Translation: Lord, give us peace in these our days.

This round can also be sung at the interval of a fourth, starting at number 2, or on the third beat of the first measure.

Debka Hora

Israeli

La la la la la la la la, La la la la la la la la.

La la la la la la la la la, La la la la la la la la.

A rhythmical Israeli dance.

Derrie Ding, Ding, Dasson

Melismata, 1611

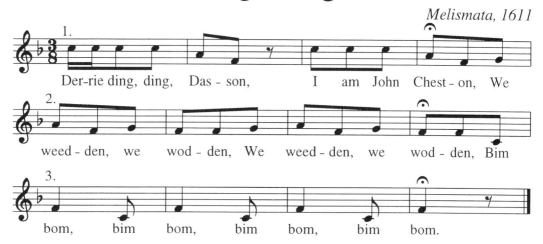

Der-rie ding, ding, Das - son, I am John Chest - on, We

weed - den, we wod - den, We weed - den, we wod - den, Bim

bom, bim bom, bim bom, bim bom.

Ding, Dong*

Ding, dong, ding, dong, Hear the morn-ing church bell play,

Hear it sound at break of day: Good day! Good day!

See La Cloche for French text.

Dona Nobis Pacem*

Do - na no - bis pa - cem, pa - cem,

do - na ___ no - bis pa - cem,

Do - na no - bis pa - cem, do - na

no - bis pa - cem, Do - na

no - bis ___ pa - cem, do - na no - bis pa - cem.

Translation: Give us peace.

Do, Re, Mi, Fa*

The School Round Book, 1852

Do, re, mi, fa,

I'm quite tired of this sol - fa - ing, I've for - got all you've been say - ing.

Early to Bed

Attributed to
Benjamin Franklin

The School Round Book, 1852

1. Ear - ly to bed and ear - ly to rise,
2. Makes a man health-y and wealth-y and wise,
3. Wise, health - y and wealth - y.

Ev'ning Still*

German

1. Ev' - ning still ___ and star - light pale,
2. By the brook ___ a night - in - gale,
3. Sad - ly his sing-ing soft - ly is wing-ing through the vale.

Farewell, Dear*

Fare - well, dear, Peace be with thee!

When I'm gone, Then ___ think of me.

See *God Bless All* and *Laugh, Ha, Ha* for alternate texts and musical variants.

Flow'rs are Dying

Flow'rs are dy - ing, Au - tumn winds are sigh - ing, sigh - ing. _

For Health and Strength

For health and strength, and dai - ly food, We praise Thy name, O Lord.

For Thy Gracious Blessings*

For thy gra - cious bless - ings, For thy won-drous word,

For thy lov - ing kind - ness, We give thanks, O Lord.

For Us a Child is Born

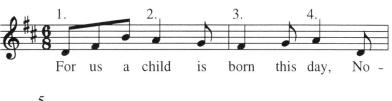

For us a child is born this day, No -

el, _____ No - el, No - el, No - el, No - el.

Glory to God*

E. Bolkovac   Ludwig Ernst Gebhardt (1787–1862)

Glo - ry to God in the high - est!

Glo - ry to God in the high - est, And _

peace on the earth, good _ will to all. A -

- men, A - men.

God Bless All*

God bless all good friends here, A
Mer - ry, Mer - ry Christ-mas and a Hap - py New Year!

See Farewell, Dear and Laugh, Ha, Ha for alternate texts and musical variants.

Good Night, Slumber Sound*

Good night, slum - ber sound, In
peace pro-found, Till morn - ing's light.

Good Night, Stars Our Light

Good night, stars our light, Dark-ness guard us thro' the night.

Good Night to You All

Good night to you all and sweet be your sleep,

May si - lence sur - round you, your slum - ber be deep,

Good night, good night, good night, good night.

Spanish text:	Adios, amigos, que duermen muy bien.
	Que vengan los angeles para guardar.
	Adios, adios, adios, adios.
Translation:	Farewell, my friends, may you sleep well.
	May the angels come to guard you. Farewell.

Go to Joan Glover*

Deuteromelia, 1609

Go to Joan Glo - ver, and tell her I love her, And

at the mid of the moon I will come to her.

The phrase "at the mid of the moon" is the original text from *Deuteromelia, 1609*. Some versions use the words "by the light of the moon."

The Great Bells of Oesney

Deuteromelia, 1609

1. The great bells of Oes - ney,
2. They ring, they sing, they ring, they sing,
3. The ten - or of them go'th mer - ri - ly.

Great Tom is Cast*

Henry Lawes (1595–1662)

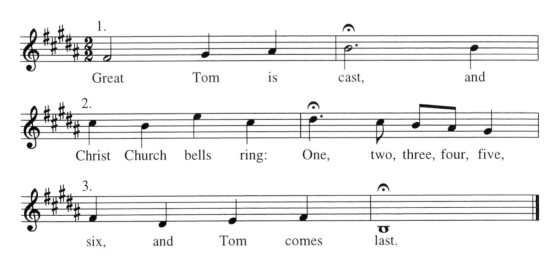

1. Great Tom is cast, and
2. Christ Church bells ring: One, two, three, four, five,
3. six, and Tom comes last.

Tom is the name of the largest bell at Christ Church, Oxford.

The Hart, He Loves the High Wood*

c. 1680

1. The hart, he loves the high wood,
2. The hare, he loves the hill,
3. The knight, he loves the bright sword,
4. The la - dy loves her will.

Hashivenu*

Israeli

1. Ha - shi - ve - nu, _ Ha - shi - ve - nu, _ Ha - shem e -
ley - cha V' - na - shu - va,
2. V' - na - shu - va, Cha - desh,
3. cha - desh ya - me - nu k' ke - dem.

Translation: Take us back to you, Lord, and we shall return. Renew our days as in the past.
See *Alleluia* for variant with alternate text.

Haste Thee, Nymph*

John Milton (1608–1674)

Samuel Arnold (1740–1802)
Catch that Catch Can, 18th C.

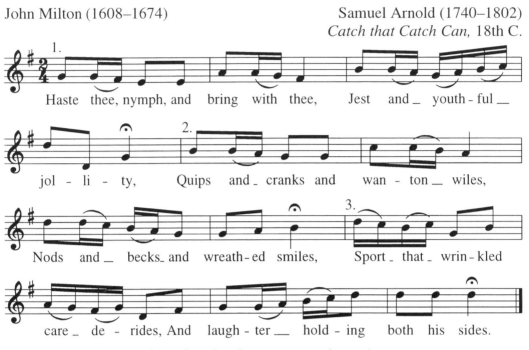

Haste thee, nymph, and bring with thee, Jest and youth-ful jol-li-ty, Quips and cranks and wan-ton wiles, Nods and becks and wreath-ed smiles, Sport that wrin-kled care de-rides, And laugh-ter hold-ing both his sides.

quips and cranks: clever, smart or witty sayings
wanton wiles: lewd, amorous tricks
beck: bow or curtsey

Hava Nashira*

Israeli

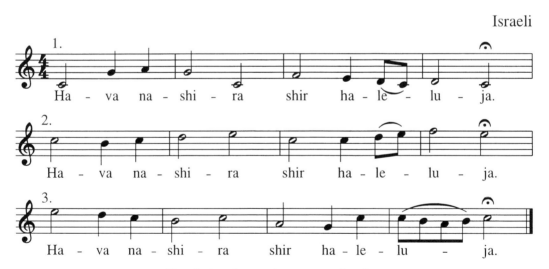

Ha - va na - shi - ra shir ha - le - lu - ja.

Ha - va na - shi - ra shir ha - le - lu - ja.

Ha - va na - shi - ra shir ha - le - lu - ja.

Translation: Let us sing a song of praise.
See *Come, Let's Be Singing* for alternate text in English.

Hear the Raindrops Fall

E. Bolkovac

Luigi Cherubini (1760–1842)

Hear the rain-drops fall, ___ Like a voice they call, ___
Urg - ing me to go ___ From this land I know, ___
To a place that's far, ___ Like some dis - tant star, ___
Shall I go and fol - low, Shall I leave to - mor - row?

Henay Ma Tov

Psalm 133:1

Traditional Israeli

He-nay ma tov hu'-ma na - im she-vet a-chim gam ya - chad.

He - nay ma ___ tov she-vet a-chim gam ya - chad.

Translation: It is so good and pleasant when brothers are together.

Here's a Health*

The School Round Book, 1852

1. Here's a health to all them that we love!
2. Here's a health to all them that love us!
3. Here's a health to all them that love those that love them!
4. Love those that love them that love us!

Hey, Ho, Nobody at Home*

Pammelia, 1609

1. Hey, ho,
2. no - bod - y at home,
3. Meat nor drink nor
4. mon - ey have I none,
5. Fill the pot, Fad - ie.

Hey, Ho, Nobody Home*
(Variant)

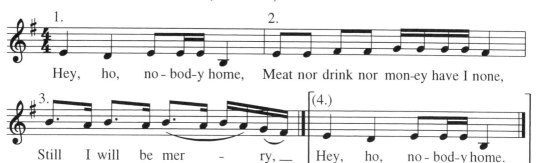

Hey, ho, no-bod-y home, Meat nor drink nor mon-ey have I none,

Still I will be mer - ry, — Hey, ho, no-bod-y home.

This is a three-part round. To sing this round as part of a quodlibet with *Ah, Poor Bird* and/or *Rose, Rose,* add the optional fourth measure in brackets.

The Higher the Plum Tree

William Lawes (1602–1645)

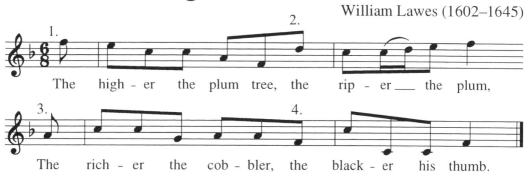

The high - er the plum tree, the rip - er — the plum,

The rich - er the cob - bler, the black - er his thumb.

Ho! Every Sleeper Waken*

Ho! ev' - ry sleep-er wak - en! The sun is in the sky,

Come, rise, — come, rise — and hear the cuck-oo cry:

Cuck - oo, cuck - oo, wake up, be spry!

Hot Mutton Pies*

The Catch Club, 1762

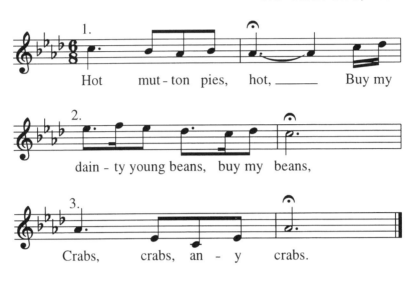

Hot mut-ton pies, hot, _____ Buy my

dain-ty young beans, buy my beans,

Crabs, crabs, an-y crabs.

Old English street cries.

I Am Athirst*

Pammelia, 1609

I am a-thirst, what should I say, A-

las, I have no mon-ey to pay, Fill the pot but-ler,

fill, fill, For I will drink with a good will.

If You Dance

If you dance then you must have boots of shin-ing leath - er,
Mon - ey in your pock - et book, in your cap a feath - er,
But if you will come with me, You don't need a
cent you see, Come and sing to - geth - er.

If You Trust

The Catch Club, 1762

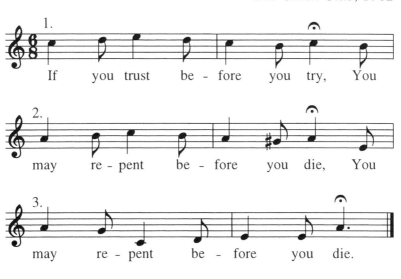

If you trust be - fore you try, You
may re - pent be - fore you die, You
may re - pent be - fore you die.

Illumina Oculos Meos

Giovanni di Palestrina (1525–1594)

Translation: Enlighten my eyes lest I sleep in death.

Joan, Come Kiss Me Now

Pammelia, 1609

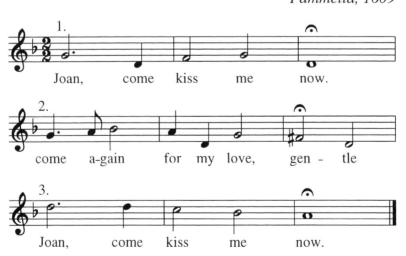

Joy in the Gates of Jerusalem*

Pammelia, 1609

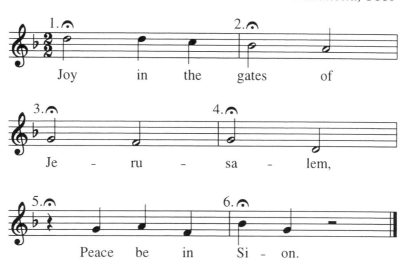

Jubilate Deo*

Michael Praetorius (1571–1621)

Translation: Rejoice in God.

Kyrie Eleison*

Translation: Lord have mercy.

La Cloche*

Translation: Ding, dong, ding, dong. This is the bell of morning
which rings at the break of day. Good day!

See *Ding, Dong* for paraphrased English text.

Lady, Come Down and See

Pammelia, 1609

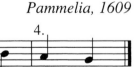

This version has been transcribed from the original notation of *Pammelia, 1609,* by Ravenscroft.

Laugh, Ha, Ha*

Laugh, ha, ha! Here's a mer - ry jest,

But if you will laugh last, You will laugh best.

See *Farewell, Dear* and *God Bless All* for alternate texts and musical variants.

Laughing, Singing

Cesar Bresgan (1913–1988)

Laugh - ing, sing - ing, laugh - ing, sing - ing

go the child - ren o - ver the hill, la, la, la, la, la, la, la,

la, la, la, la, la, la, la o - ver the hill.

Let's Put the Rooster in the Stew

Let's put the roost - er in the stew,

Let's put the roost - er in the stew,

Then he can - not sing cock - a - doo - dle, doo - dle - doo,

Then he can - not sing cock - a - doo - dle, doo - dle - doo.

This is an English version of *Mon Coq est Mort.*

TXB-86

Let's Sing Till Echoes Ring

Let's sing till ech-oes ring: Fa, la, la, la, la! _____

Let Us Sing Together*

Let us sing to-geth - er, Let us sing to-geth - er, One and all a
joy - ous song, Let us sing to - geth - er, One and all a
joy - ous song, Let us sing a - gain and a - gain,
Let us sing a - gain and a - gain, Let us sing a -
gain and a - gain, One and all a joy - ous song.

Like a Bird

E. Bolkovac

Luigi Cherubini (1760–1842)

Like a bird up in the sky, I'd like to soar with the sky an o - pen door, With-out rea - son with-out why, Just to fly up in the sky, To feel I'm free with noth-ing stop-ping me, To fly up in the sky!

The Little Bell at Westminster

The lit - tle bell at West-min-ster goes ding, dong, ding, dong, dong.

London's Burning

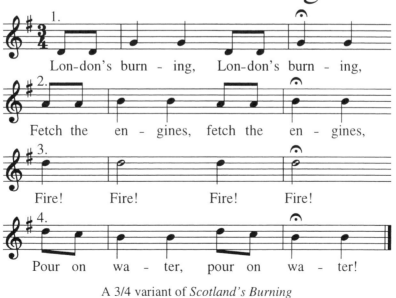

Lon-don's burn - ing, Lon-don's burn - ing,

Fetch the en - gines, fetch the en - gines,

Fire! Fire! Fire! Fire!

Pour on wa - ter, pour on wa - ter!

A 3/4 variant of Scotland's Burning

TXB-86

Lord, Hear Our Prayer*

E. Bolkovac

Franz Joseph Haydn (1732–1809)

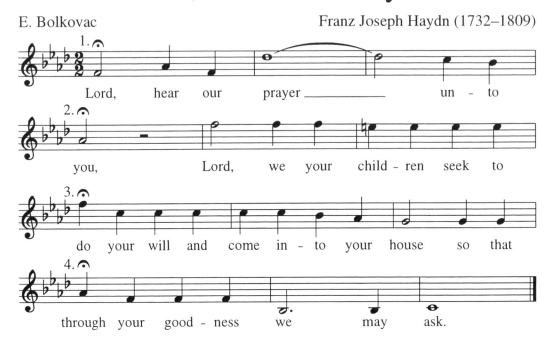

Lord, hear our prayer _____ un - to you, Lord, we your child - ren seek to do your will and come in - to your house so that through your good - ness we may ask.

Lo Yissa Goy

Isaiah 2:4
Micah 4:3

Israeli

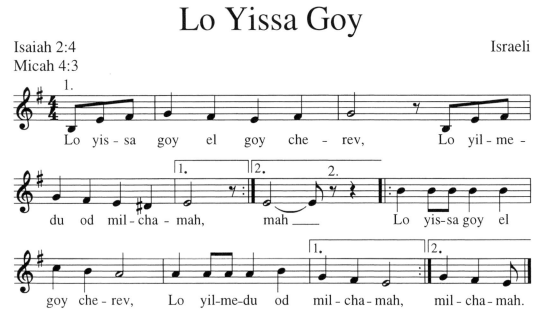

Lo yis - sa goy el goy che - rev, Lo yil - me - du od mil - cha - mah, mah _____ Lo yis - sa goy el goy che - rev, Lo yil - me - du od mil - cha - mah, mil - cha - mah.

Translation: Nations will not raise their swords against nations. They will no longer study war.
See *Vine and Fig Tree* for paraphrased English text.

Make New Friends*

Margery, Serve Well the Black Sow*

Deuteromelia, 1609

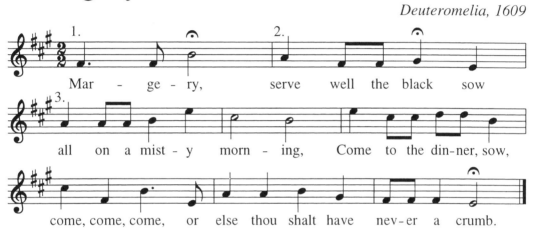

Miserere Nobis, Domine

William Byrd (1541–1623)

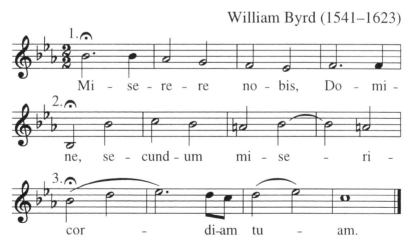

Translation: Lord, have mercy on us according to your kindness.

TXB-86

Mon Coq est Mort*

Translation: My rooster is dead. He will no longer say: cockadoodle doo.
This is a French version of *Let's Put the Rooster in the Stew.*

Morning is Come*

William H. Bradbury (1816–1868)

My Dame Hath a Lame, Tame Crane*

Matthew White (fl. 1600–1630)

1. My dame hath a lame, tame crane,
2. My dame hath a crane that is lame,
3. Good gen - tle Jane, let my dame's lame, tame
4. crane feed and come home a - gain.

My Dame Had a Lame, Tame Crane*
(Variant)

1. My Dame had a lame, tame crane,
2. My Dame had a crane that was lame.
3. Oh pray, gen - tle Jane, let my Dame's lame, tame
4. crane drink and come home a - gain.

My Paddle

Words & Music by Margaret McGee, 1918

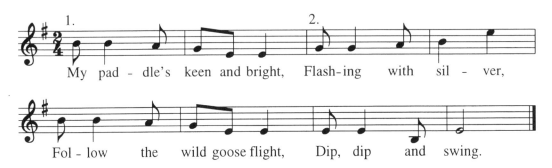

My pad - dle's keen and bright, Flash-ing with sil - ver,

Fol - low the wild goose flight, Dip, dip and swing.

Now All the Woods are Waking

Words & Music by Max Exner

Now all the woods are wak - ing, the sun is ris - ing high,

Wake up now, get up now, be - fore the dew is dry.

Now Good Night

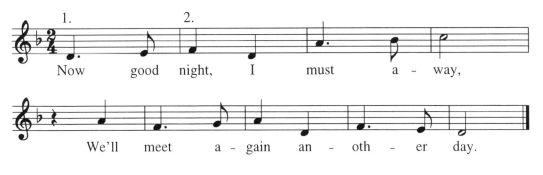

Now good night, I must a - way,

We'll meet a - gain an - oth - er day.

Now Kiss the Cup

Pammelia, 1609

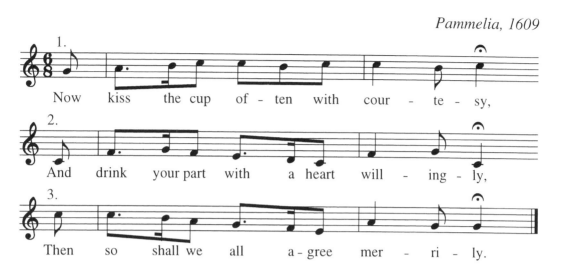

1. Now kiss the cup of - ten with cour - te - sy,

2. And drink your part with a heart will - ing - ly,

3. Then so shall we all a - gree mer - ri - ly.

Oh, How Lovely is the Evening

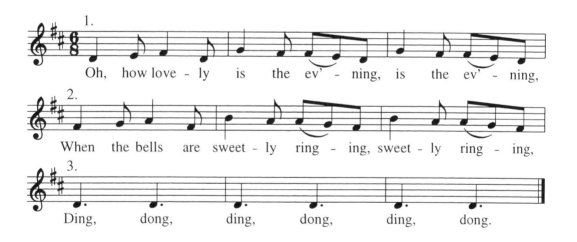

1. Oh, how love - ly is the ev' - ning, is the ev' - ning,

2. When the bells are sweet - ly ring - ing, sweet - ly ring - ing,

3. Ding, dong, ding, dong, ding, dong.

Oh, How Sweet

1. Oh, how 2. sweet, how 3. sweet _ is our 4. sing - ing.

Oh, My Love*

Deuteromelia, 1609

Oh, my love, Lov'st thou me? Then quick-ly come and save him that dies for thee.

This round also works well in minor. A minor version of *Oh, My Love*, can be found in *The Catch Club, 1762.*

One May Begin*

Moritz Hauptmann (1792–1868)

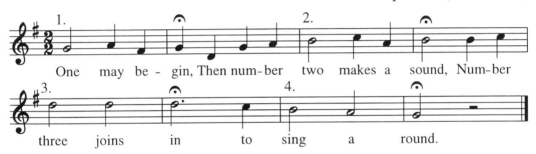

One may be-gin, Then num-ber two makes a sound, Num-ber three joins in to sing a round.

O Nightingale*

Philip James (1890–1975)

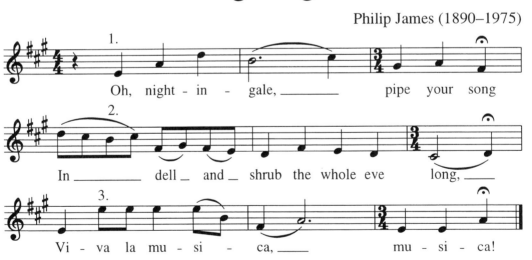

Oh, night-in-gale, _____ pipe your song In _____ dell _ and _ shrub the whole eve long, _____ Vi - va la mu-si - ca, _____ mu-si-ca!

Viva la musica: Long live music!

Pauper Sum Ego

Pau-per sum e - go, Ni - hil ha - be - o, Cor me-um da - bo.

Translation: I am poor. I have nothing. I will give my heart.

Please Bless Our Food*

E. Bolkovac

Antonio Caldara (1670–1736)

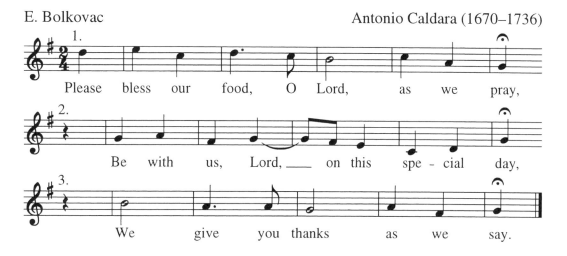

Please bless our food, O Lord, as we pray,

Be with us, Lord, __ on this spe - cial day,

We give you thanks as we say.

Poor Tom*

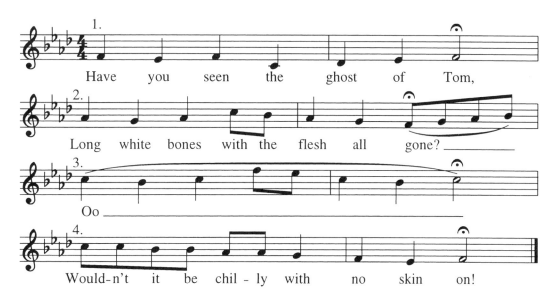

Have you seen the ghost of Tom,

Long white bones with the flesh all gone? __

Oo __

Would-n't it be chil - ly with no skin on!

TXB-86

42

Rise Up, O Flame

Christoph Praetorius (d. 1609)

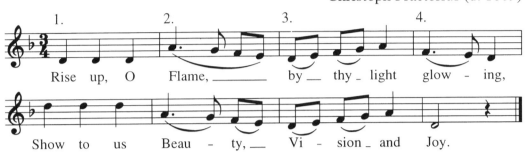

Rise up, O Flame, ___ by ___ thy ___ light glow - ing,

Show to us Beau - ty, ___ Vi - sion ___ and Joy.

This text for *Rise Up, O Flame* is a translation of Fritz Jöde's text found in his collection *Der Kanon. Rise Up, O Flame* may be sung as part of a quodlibet with *There Is No Sorrow.*

Rose, Rose*

Rose, Rose, Rose, Rose, Will I ev - er see thee red?

Aye, mar - ry that I will, if thou but stay.

This is an English variant of *Beaux Yeux.* Some versions use: "Will I ever see thee wed?" This round may be sung as part of a quodlibet with *Ah, Poor Bird* and/or *Hey, Ho, Nobody Home (Variant).*

Row, Row, Row Your Boat*

Row, row, row your boat,

Gen - tly down the stream,

Mer - ri - ly, mer - ri - ly, mer - ri - ly, mer - ri - ly,

Life is but a dream.

TXB-86

Row the Boat, Whittington

The Catch Club, 1762

Row the boat, Whit-ting-ton, Thou wor-thy cit - i-zen, Lord Mayor of Lon-don.

Scotland's Burning*

Scot - land's burn - ing, Scot - land's burn - ing,

Fetch the en - gines, Fetch the en - gines, Fire! fire!

fire! fire! Pour on wa - ter, Pour on wa - ter.

This round is a 2/4 variant of *London's Burning.*

See the Star of Bethlehem

Seymour Batab   Louis Haber

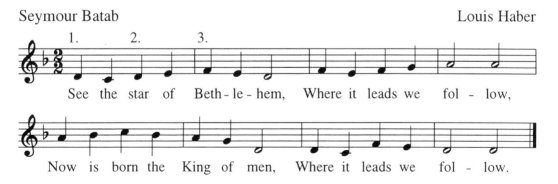

See the star of Beth - le - hem, Where it leads we fol - low,

Now is born the King of men, Where it leads we fol - low.

From ***THE SEASON FOR SINGING*** by John Langstaff. Copyright © 1974 by John Langstaff.
Used by permission of Doubleday, a division of Bantam Doubleday Dell Publishing Group, Inc.

Shalom Chaverim

Israeli

Translation: Goodbye, friends! See you again, goodbye!
See *Shalom, My Friends* for paraphrased English text.

Shalom, My Friends

Israeli

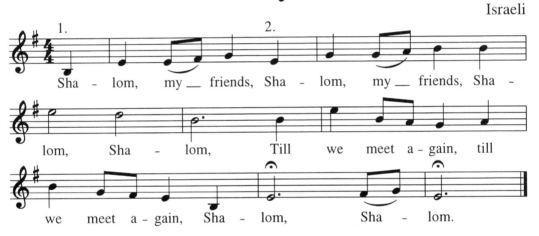

Sing and Rejoice*

William Bradbury (1816–1868)

Sing, Sing Together

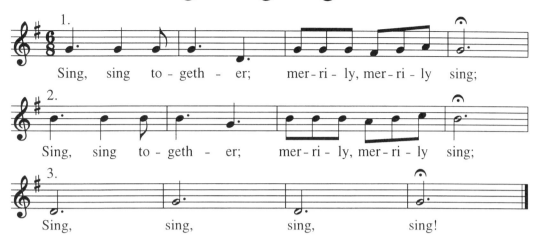

Sing, sing to-geth-er; mer-ri-ly, mer-ri-ly sing;

Sing, sing to-geth-er; mer-ri-ly, mer-ri-ly sing;

Sing, sing, sing, sing!

Sing With Us*

Antonio Caldara (1670–1736)

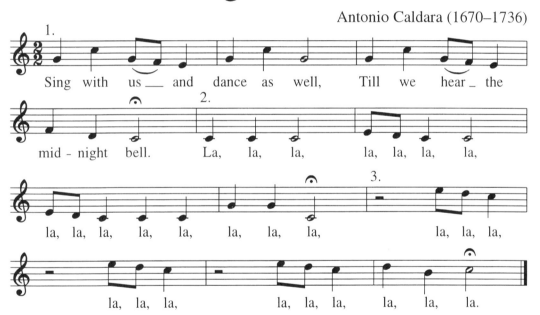

Sing with us and dance as well, Till we hear the

mid-night bell. La, la, la, la, la, la, la,

la, la, la, la, la, la, la, la, la, la, la,

la, la, la, la, la, la, la, la, la.

Sleep, Sleep, My Jesus*

Sleep, sleep, my Je - sus ba - by, go to sleep.

Alternate text: Sleep, sleep, my lit-tle ba-by, go to sleep.

TXB-86

The Swan*

Sweet-ly the swan sings: do, de, ah, do, do, de, ah, do, do, de, ah, do.

Sweet Sings the Nightingale*

Pammelia, 1609

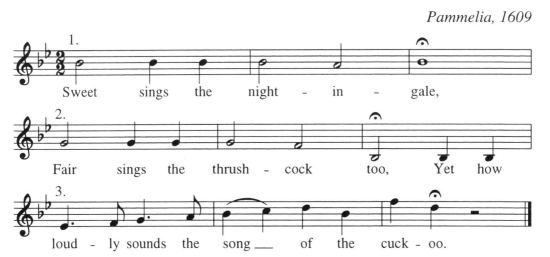

1. Sweet sings the night - in - gale,

2. Fair sings the thrush - cock too, Yet how

3. loud - ly sounds the song __ of the cuck - oo.

This text has been adapted from the original found in *Pammelia, 1609.*

Sweetly Sings the Donkey

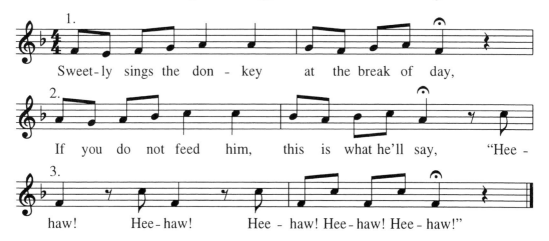

1. Sweet-ly sings the don - key at the break of day,

2. If you do not feed him, this is what he'll say, "Hee -

3. haw! Hee - haw! Hee - haw! Hee - haw! Hee - haw!"

There is No Sorrow*

Words & Music by Robert Burrell (1956–   )

There is no sor - row

like the___ lone - ly,

there is ___ no ___ suf - f'ring like

those with - out love.

This round may be sung as part of a quodlibet with *Rise Up, O Flame.*

There Was an Old Fellow

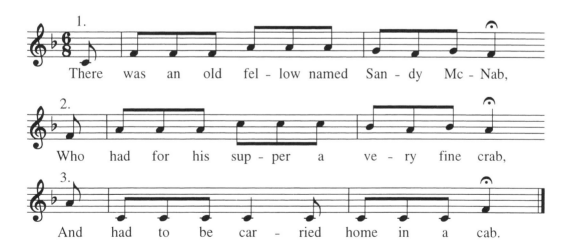

There was an old fel - low named San - dy Mc - Nab,

Who had for his sup - per a ve - ry fine crab,

And had to be car - ried home in a cab.

48

Three Blind Mice*

Deuteromelia, 1609

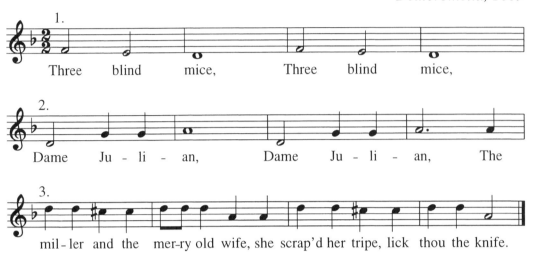

1. Three blind mice, Three blind mice,
2. Dame Ju - li - an, Dame Ju - li - an, The
3. mil - ler and the mer-ry old wife, she scrap'd her tripe, lick thou the knife.

Three Blind Mice*
(Variant)

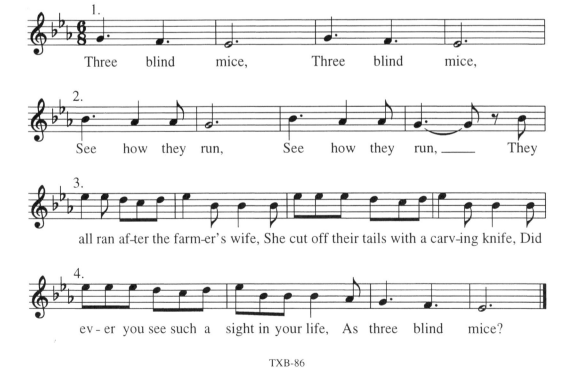

1. Three blind mice, Three blind mice,
2. See how they run, See how they run, _____ They
3. all ran af-ter the farm-er's wife, She cut off their tails with a carv-ing knife, Did
4. ev - er you see such a sight in your life, As three blind mice?

TXB-86

Through North and South

William Billings (1746–1800)

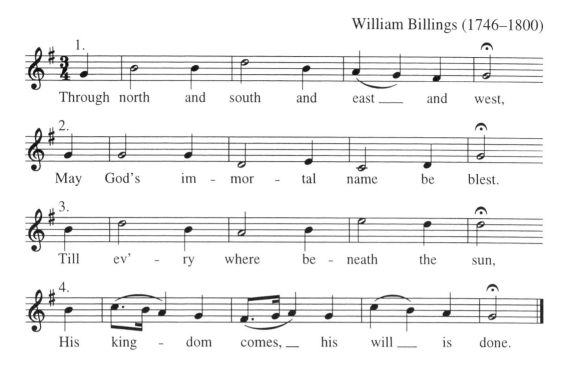

Through north and south and east ___ and west,

May God's im - mor - tal name be blest.

Till ev' - ry where be - neath the sun,

His king - dom comes, ___ his will ___ is done.

Toembai*

Israeli

Toem-bai, toem-bai, toem-bai, toem-bai, toem-bai, toem-bai, toem - bai,

Tra - la - la, la, la, la, la, la, la, la, la, la, la, la,

Tra - la-la, la, la, la, la, la, la, la, la, la, la, la, la, la.

'Toembai' is an Israeli nonsense word.

TXB-86

To Portsmouth*

Pammelia, 1609

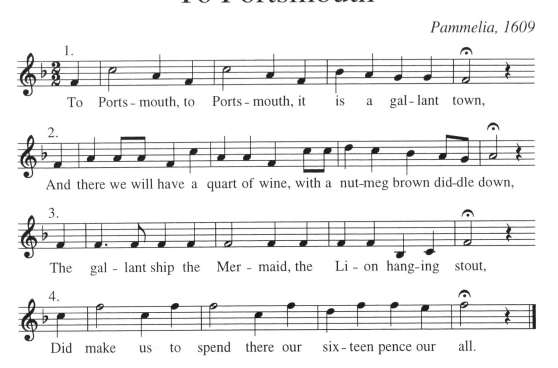

1. To Ports-mouth, to Ports-mouth, it is a gal-lant town,

2. And there we will have a quart of wine, with a nut-meg brown did-dle down,

3. The gal-lant ship the Mer-maid, the Li-on hang-ing stout,

4. Did make us to spend there our six-teen pence our all.

Ubi Sunt Gaudia*

Philip Hayes (1738–1797)

1. U-bi sunt gau-di-a 2. in heav-en there an-gels sing,

3. No-va can-ti-ca and 4. al-le-lu-ias ring, In

5. re-gis cu-ri-a 6. gau-di-um est!

Translation: Where there is joy, there angels sing new songs in heaven, and alleluias ring.
In the courts of the King there is joy.

TXB-86

Vine and Fig Tree

Israeli

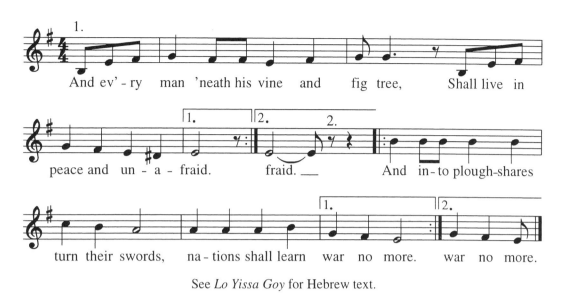

And ev'-ry man 'neath his vine and fig tree, Shall live in peace and un - a - fraid. fraid. And in-to plough-shares turn their swords, na-tions shall learn war no more. war no more.

See *Lo Yissa Goy* for Hebrew text.

Viva la Musica

Michael Praetorius (1571–1621)

Vi - va, vi - va la mu - si - ca,

Vi - va, vi - va la mu - si - ca,

Vi - va la mu - si - ca!

Translation: Long live music!

TXB-86

Welcome All

E. Bolkovac

Franz Joseph Haydn (1732–1809)

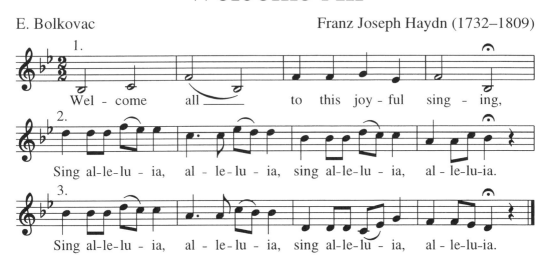

Wel - come all ___ to this joy - ful sing - ing,

Sing al-le-lu - ia, al - le-lu - ia, sing al-le-lu - ia, al - le-lu-ia.

Sing al-le-lu - ia, al - le-lu - ia, sing al-le-lu - ia, al - le-lu-ia.

Alternate texts for first line:
Christ is risen on this joyful morning.
Christ is born on this joyful morning.

Welcome, Every Guest*

Knoxville Harmony, 1838

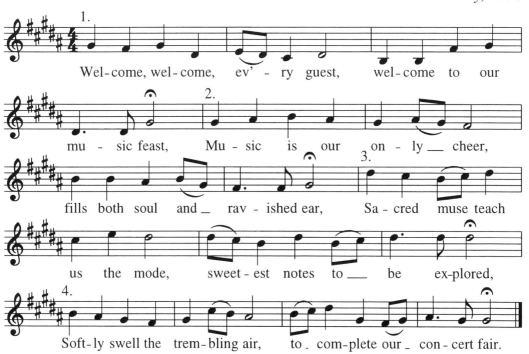

Wel-come, wel-come, ev' - ry guest, wel-come to our

mu - sic feast, Mu - sic is our on - ly ___ cheer,

fills both soul and ___ rav - ished ear, Sa - cred muse teach

us the mode, sweet-est notes to ___ be ex-plored,

Soft-ly swell the trem-bling air, to ___ com-plete our ___ con - cert fair.

We Thank Thee for Our Daily Bread

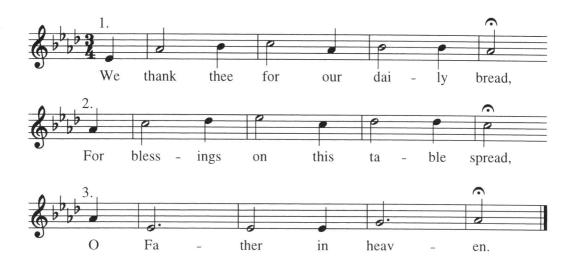

Where is John?

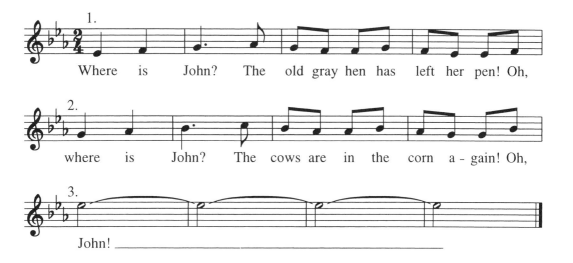

Whistle, Daughter

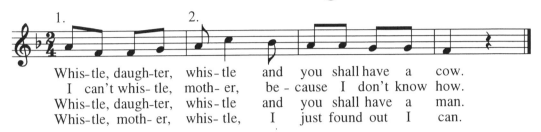

Whis-tle, daugh-ter, whis-tle and you shall have a cow.
I can't whis-tle, moth-er, be-cause I don't know how.
Whis-tle, daugh-ter, whis-tle and you shall have a man.
Whis-tle, moth-er, whis-tle, I just found out I can.

The White Hen*

Pammelia, 1609

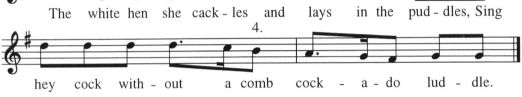

The white hen she cack-les and lays in the pud-dles, Sing hey cock with-out a comb cock-a-do lud-dle.

White Sand and Grey Sand

Apollonian Harmony, 1790

White sand and grey sand,

Who'll buy my grey sand?

Who'll buy my white sand?

Old English street cry.

TXB-86

Why Shouldn't My Goose?

1. Why should-n't my goose,

2. Sing as well as thy goose?

3. When I paid for my goose,

4. Twice as much as thou?

With Laughter and Singing

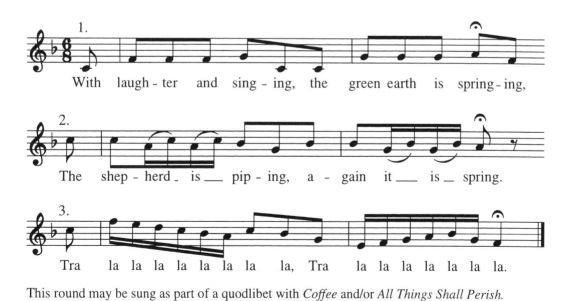

1. With laugh-ter and sing-ing, the green earth is spring-ing,

2. The shep-herd is pip-ing, a-gain it is spring.

3. Tra la la la la la la la la, Tra la la la la la la la.

This round may be sung as part of a quodlibet with *Coffee* and/or *All Things Shall Perish.*

1.

2.

3.

Hungarian

4.

Russian

5.

Hungarian

6.

Franz Joseph Haydn (1732–1809)

7.

Hungarian

8.

9.

10.

58

59

from *Piae Cantiones, 1582*

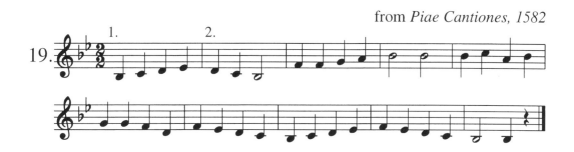

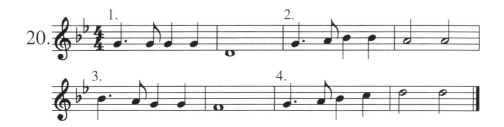

TXB-86

ADD YOUR OWN ROUNDS

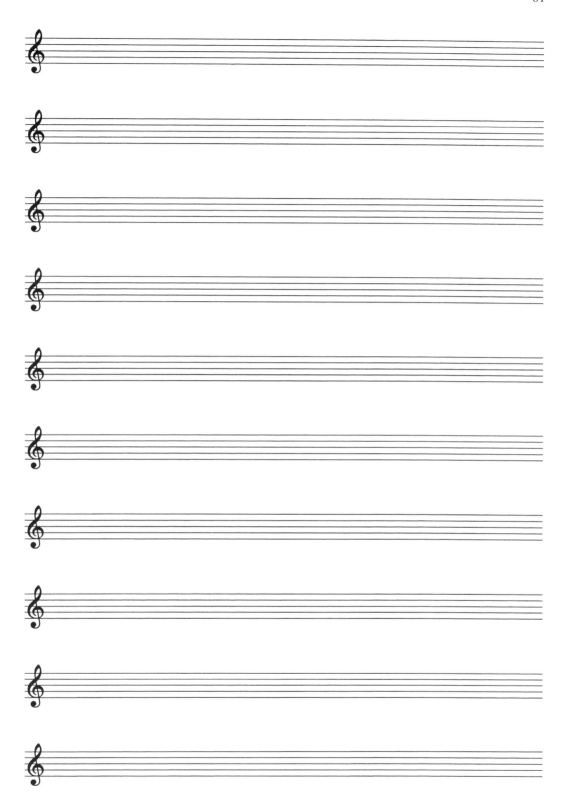

Selected Rounds in Score Format

Adiuva Nos, Deus

Pammelia, 1609

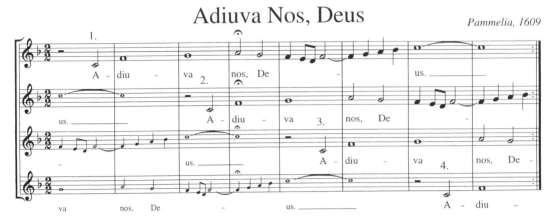

Ah, Poor Bird

Alleluia

Israeli

All into Service

Pammelia, 1609

A Ram Sam Sam

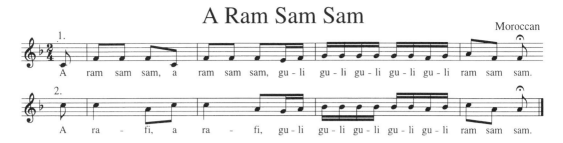

At Summer Morn

Beaux Yeux

The Bell Doth Toll

TXB-86

The Birch Tree

Russian

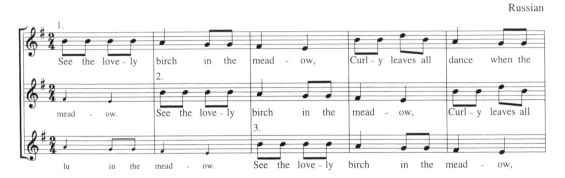

See the love-ly birch in the mead - ow, Curl - y leaves all dance when the

mead - ow. See the love-ly birch in the mead - ow, Curl - y leaves all

lu in the mead - ow. See the love-ly birch in the mead - ow,

wind blows, Lu - li, lu - li, the wind blows, Lu - li, lu in the mead-ow.

dance when the wind blows, Lu - li, lu - li, the wind blows, Lu - li, lu in the

Curl-y leaves all dance when the wind blows, Lu - li, lu - li, the wind blows, Lu - li,

Chairs to Mend

William Hayes (1706–1777)

Chairs to mend, old chairs to mend,

Mack - er - el, fresh mack - er - el, An - y

old rags, An - y old rags?

Cherries So Ripe

Cher - ries so ripe and so round, The

best in the mar - ket found,

On - ly a pen - ny a pound,

Who will buy?

Coffee

Elinor O'Connor

Karl Gottlieb Hering (1766–1853)

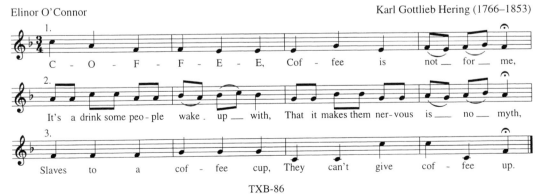

C - O - F - F - E - E, Cof - fee is not for me,

It's a drink some peo - ple wake up with, That it makes them ner-vous is no myth,

Slaves to a cof - fee cup, They can't give cof - fee up.

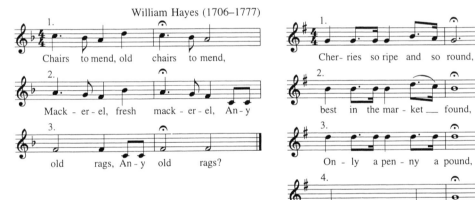

Come Follow

John Hilton (1599–1657)

1. Come fol-low, fol-low, fol-low, fol-low, fol-low, fol-low me!

2. Whith-er shall I fol-low, fol-low, fol-low, whith-er shall I fol-low, fol-low thee?

3. To the green-wood, to the green-wood, to the green-wood, green - wood tree.

Dame, Lend Me a Loaf

Pammelia, 1609

1. Dame, lend me a loaf, Dame, lend me a loaf from

2. Sat-ur-day to Sat-ur-day and long-er if you long-er may,

3. Dame, lend me a loaf, Dame, lend me a loaf.

Da Pacem, Domine

Melchior Franck (1573–1639)

1. Da pa-cem, Do-mi-ne, da pa-cem, Do-mi-ne, in di-e-bus nos - tris.

2. bus nos - tris. Da pa-cem, Do-mi-ne, da pa-cem, Do-mi-ne, in di-e-

Ding, Dong

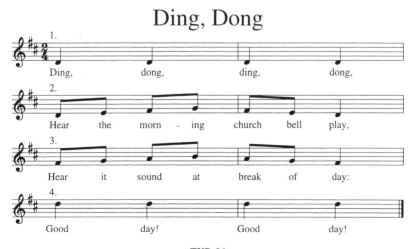

1. Ding, dong, ding, dong,

2. Hear the morn-ing church bell play,

3. Hear it sound at break of day:

4. Good day! Good day!

TXB-86

Dona Nobis Pacem

Dona nobis pacem, pacem, dona nobis pacem,
Dona nobis pacem, dona nobis pacem,
Dona nobis pacem, dona nobis pacem.

Do, Re, Mi, Fa

The School Round Book, 1852

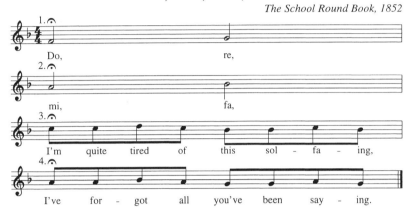

Do, re,
mi, fa,
I'm quite tired of this sol-fa-ing,
I've for-got all you've been say-ing.

Ev'ning Still

German

Ev' - ning still ____ and star - light pale,
By the brook ____ a night - in - gale,
Sad - ly his sing - ing soft - ly is wing-ing through the vale.

Farewell, Dear

Fare - well, dear,
Peace be with thee!
When I'm gone, Then ____
think of me.

For Thy Gracious Blessings

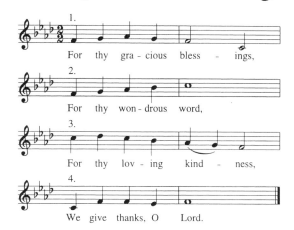

For thy gra - cious bless - ings,

For thy won - drous word,

For thy lov - ing kind - ness,

We give thanks, O Lord.

Glory to God

E. Bolkovac

Ludwig Ernst Gebhardt (1787–1862)

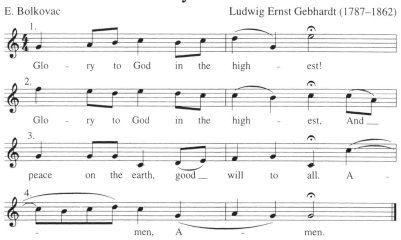

Glo - ry to God in the high - est!

Glo - ry to God in the high - est, And

peace on the earth, good will to all. A -

- men, A - men.

God Bless All

God bless all

good friends here, A

Mer - ry, Mer - ry Christ - mas and a

Hap - py New Year!

Good Night, Slumber Sound

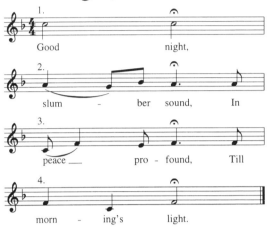

Go to Joan Glover

Deuteromelia, 1609

Great Tom is Cast

Henry Lawes (1595–1662)

The Hart, He Loves the High Wood

c. 1680

1. The hart, he loves the high wood,

2. The hare, he loves the hill,

3. The knight, he loves the bright sword,

4. The la-dy loves her will.

Hashivenu

Israeli

1. Ha-shi-ve-nu, _ Ha-shi-ve-nu, _ Ha-shem e-ley-cha

2. V'-na-shu-va, V'-na-shu-va,

3. Cha-desh, cha-desh ya-me-nu k'-ke-dem.

Haste Thee, Nymph

John Milton (1608–1674)

Samuel Arnold (1740–1802)
Catch that Catch Can, 18th C.

1. Haste thee, nymph, and bring with thee, Jest and _ youth-ful _ jol-li-ty,

2. Quips and _ cranks and wan-ton_wiles, Nods and _ becks_and wreath-ed smiles,

3. Sport_ that_ wrin-kled care_ de-rides, And laugh-ter__ hold-ing both his sides.

Hava Nashira

Israeli

1. Ha-va na-shi-ra shir ha-le-lu-ja.

2. Ha-va na-shi-ra shir ha-le-lu-ja.

3. Ha-va na-shi-ra shir ha-le-lu-ja.

TXB-86

Here's a Health

The School Round Book, 1852

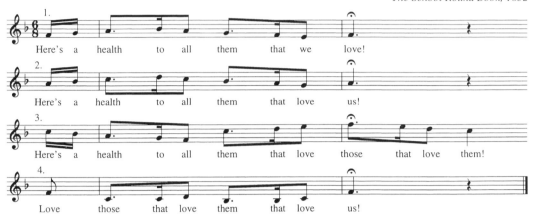

1. Here's a health to all them that we love!

2. Here's a health to all them that love us!

3. Here's a health to all them that love those that love them!

4. Love those that love them that love us!

Hey, Ho, Nobody at Home

Pammelia, 1609

1. Hey, ho,

2. no - bod - y at home,

3. Meat nor drink nor

4. mon - ey have I none,

5. Fill the pot, Fad - ie.

Hey, Ho, Nobody Home
(Variant)

1. Hey, ho, no - bod-y home,

2. Meat nor drink nor mon-ey have I none,

3. Still I will be mer - ry, —

(4.) Hey, ho, no - bod-y home.

TXB-86

Ho! Every Sleeper Waken

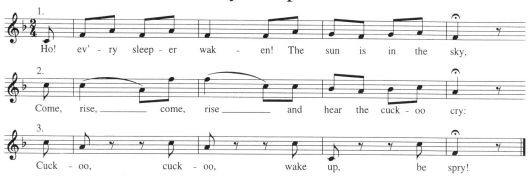

1. Ho! ev'-ry sleep-er wak-en! The sun is in the sky,

2. Come, rise, _____ come, rise _____ and hear the cuck-oo cry:

3. Cuck-oo, cuck-oo, wake up, be spry!

Hot Mutton Pies

The Catch Club, 1762

1. Hot mut-ton pies, hot, _____ Buy my

2. dain-ty young beans, buy my beans,

3. Crabs, crabs, an-y crabs.

I Am Athirst

Pammelia, 1609

1. I am a thirst, what should I say, A-las I have no mon-ey to pay,

with a good will. I am a thirst, what should I say, A-las I have no

2. For I will drink with a good will. I am a-thirst what should I say, A-

Fill the pot but-ler, fill, fill, For I will drink with a good will.

mon-ey to pay, Fill the pot but-ler, fill, fill, For I will drink

las I have no mon-ey to pay, Fill the pot but-ler, fill, fill,

Joy in the Gates of Jerusalem

Pammelia, 1609

Jubilate Deo

Michael Praetorius (1571–1621)

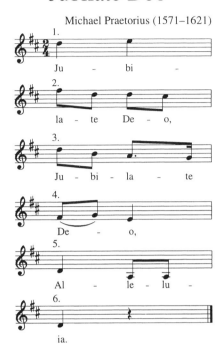

Kyrie Eleison

La Cloche

Laugh, Ha, Ha

Laugh, ha, ha!

Here's a mer - ry jest,

But if you will laugh last,

You will laugh best.

Let Us Sing Together

Let us sing to-geth - er, Let us sing to-geth - er, One and all a joy - ous song,

Let us sing to - geth - er, One and all a joy - ous song,

Let us sing a - gain and a-gain, Let us sing a - gain and a - gain,

Let us sing a - gain and a - gain, One and all a joy - ous song.

Lord, Hear Our Prayer

E. Bolkovac

Franz Joseph Haydn (1732–1809)

Lord, hear our prayer _____ un - to

you, Lord, we your child - ren seek to

do your will and come in - to your house so that

through your good - ness we may ask.

Make New Friends

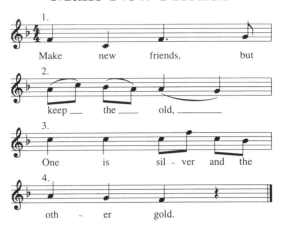

Make new friends, but
keep the old,
One is sil-ver and the
oth-er gold.

Margery, Serve Well the Black Sow

Deuteromelia, 1609

Mon Coq est Mort

Morning is Come

William H. Bradbury (1816–1868)

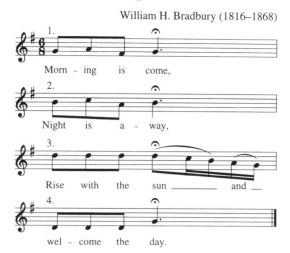

1. Morn - ing is come,

2. Night is a - way,

3. Rise with the sun _____ and _____

4. wel - come the day.

My Dame Hath a Lame, Tame Crane

Matthew White (fl. 1600–1630)

1. My dame hath a lame, tame crane,

2. My dame hath a crane that is lame,

3. Good gen - tle Jane, let my dame's lame, tame

4. crane feed and come home a - gain.

My Dame Had a Lame, Tame Crane

(Variant)

1. My Dame had a lame, tame crane,

2. My Dame had a crane that was lame.

3. Oh pray, gen - tle Jane, let my Dame's lame, tame

4. crane drink and come home a - gain.

Oh, My Love

Deuteromelia, 1609

1. Oh, my love,
2. Lov'st thou me? Then
3. quick - ly come and save him that
4. dies for thee.

One May Begin

Moritz Hauptmann (1792–1868)

1. One may be - gin, Then num - ber
2. two makes a sound, Num - ber
3. three joins in to
4. sing a round.

O Nightingale

Philip James (1890–1975)

1. Oh, night - in - gale, _____ pipe your song
2. In _____ dell _ and _ shrub the whole eve long, _____
3. Vi - va la mu - si - ca, _____ mu - si - ca!

Please Bless Our Food

E. Bolkovac

Antonio Caldara (1670–1736)

1. Please bless our food, O Lord, as we pray,

2. Be with us, Lord, on this spe - cial day,

3. We give you thanks as we say.

Poor Tom

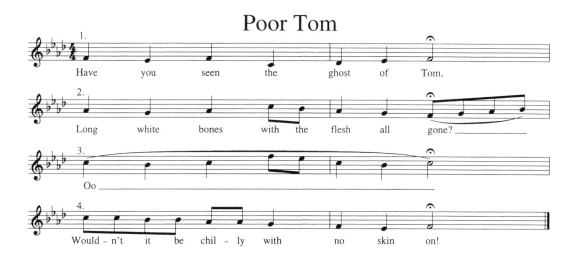

1. Have you seen the ghost of Tom,

2. Long white bones with the flesh all gone?

3. Oo

4. Would - n't it be chil - ly with no skin on!

Rose, Rose

1. Rose, Rose, Rose, Rose,

2. Will I ev - er see thee red?

3. Aye, mar - ry that I will,

4. if thou but stay.

Row, Row, Row Your Boat

Scotland's Burning

Sing and Rejoice

William Bradbury (1816–1868)

Sing With Us

Antonio Caldara (1670–1736)

Sing with us — and dance as well, Till we hear — the mid - night bell.

La, la, la, la, la, la, la, la, la, la, la, la, la, la, la, la,

la, la, la, la, la, la, la, la, la, la, la, la.

Sleep, Sleep, My Jesus

Sleep, sleep, my

Je – sus

ba – by, go _____ to

sleep. _____

The Swan

Sweet - ly the swan sings:

do, de, ah, do,

do, de, ah, do,

do, de, ah, do.

Sweet Sings the Nightingale

Pammelia, 1609

There is No Sorrow

Words & Music by Robert Burrell (1956–)

Three Blind Mice

Deuteromelia, 1609

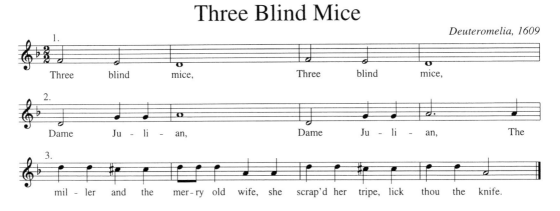

Three Blind Mice
(Variant)

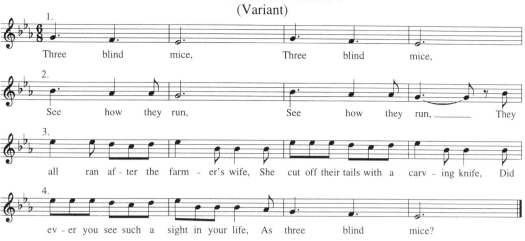

Three blind mice, Three blind mice,

See how they run, See how they run, _____ They

all ran af-ter the farm-er's wife, She cut off their tails with a carv-ing knife, Did

ev-er you see such a sight in your life, As three blind mice?

Toembai

Israeli

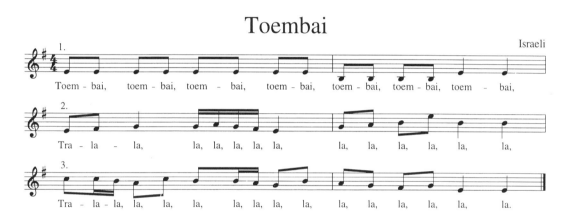

Toem-bai, toem-bai, toem-bai, toem-bai, toem-bai, toem-bai, toem-bai,

Tra-la-la, la, la, la, la, la, la, la, la, la, la,

Tra-la-la, la, la, la, la, la, la, la, la, la, la, la, la.

To Portsmouth

Pammelia, 1609

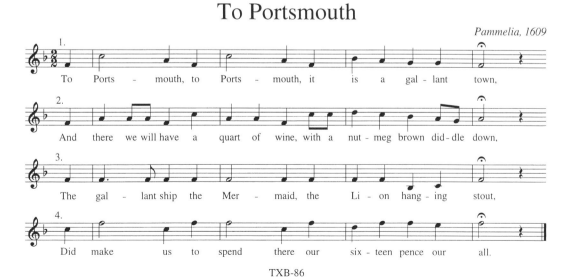

To Ports-mouth, to Ports-mouth, it is a gal-lant town,

And there we will have a quart of wine, with a nut-meg brown did-dle down,

The gal-lant ship the Mer-maid, the Li-on hang-ing stout,

Did make us to spend there our six-teen pence our all.

TXB-86

84

Ubi Sunt Gaudia

Philip Hayes (1738–1797)

U - bi sunt gau - di - a in

heav - en there an - gels sing,

No - va can - ti - ca and

al - le - lu - ias__ ring, In

re - gis cu - ri - a

gau - di - um est!

Welcome, Every Guest

Knoxville Harmony, 1838

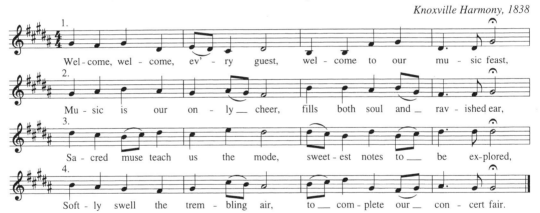

Wel - come, wel - come, ev' - ry guest, wel - come to our mu - sic feast,

Mu - sic is our on - ly__ cheer, fills both soul and__ rav - ished ear,

Sa - cred muse teach us the mode, sweet - est notes to__ be ex - plored,

Soft - ly swell the trem - bling air, to__ com - plete our__ con - cert fair.

The White Hen

Pammelia, 1609

The white hen she cack - les

and lays in the pud - dles,

Sing hey cock with - out a

comb cock - a - do lud - dle.

GENERAL CATEGORIES

ANIMALS

BELLS

88

NUMBER OF PARTS

PEDAGOGICAL CATEGORIES

Although originally conceived as a musical, not pedagogical resource, the rounds in this collection provide a wealth of material from which many musical concepts may be taught.

The lists on the following pages are not comprehensive but do suggest ways in which this collection may be utilized in music education programs. Interested teachers should analyze the rounds from a pedagogical standpoint as well, and add additional rounds to the various categories.

Meter (pages 91-92)

Teachers will find that basic time signatures are well represented, but more experienced students can be challenged by progressing to meters such as 6/4, 3/8, 3/2 and even mixed meters as in *O Nightingale*. While studying the rounds, students can learn the basic conducting patterns. Care should be taken, however, to encourage musical singing and conducting, and avoid unmusical, mechanical, and vocally detrimental motions.

Rhythmic Elements (page 93)

A small number of rounds have been selected to demonstrate their pedagogical potential in terms of rhythm. Within these rhythmic categories, however, one can also find differences in the overall difficulty with respect to melodic patterns. intervals, range, vocal difficulty, etc. Younger children, for example, may learn from *Ding, Dong, Ding, Dong*, while older children may learn the same rhythmic elements from the more difficult *Coffee*. Teachers need to decide which rounds are appropriate for the level and needs of their class.

The order of the rhythmic elements presented on page 93 does not state a required sequence, but does fit many of the sequential, developmental programs in current use.

Melodic Elements (page 93)

For purposes of melodic analysis, the system of *relative moveable do* has been used. In this system, *do* is the first scale degree in major, and *la* is the first degree in minor.

Once students in a Kodály-based music program have learned the pentatonic notes: *do, re, mi, so,* and *la*, this collection can provide useful material for teaching *fa* and *ti* and lead to the understanding of the full diatonic scale.

Teachers, conductors, and song leaders who do not wish to use this collection as part of a music literacy program may teach the rounds by rote to enrich their classroom, school or choral activities.

METER

2/4 - Without Anacrusis

2/4 - With Anacrusis

3/4 - Without Anacrusis

3/4 - With Anacrusis

4/4 - Without Anacrusis

RHYTHMIC ELEMENTS

Anacrusis

MELODIC ELEMENTS

fa

ti

fa & ti

SCALE FORMS:

Limited Range (Sixth or less)

94

MISCELLANEOUS

Introducing Harmony

PRONUNCIATION GUIDE

The following French, Hebrew and Spanish texts have been transcribed using the International Phonetic Alphabet:

A - di - os, a - mi - gos, que duer - men muy bien.
[a - di - os a - mi - gos ke dwɛr - mɛn mwi bjen

Que ven - gan los an - ge - les pa - ra guar - dar.
ke βɛn - gan los an - he - lɛs pa - ra juar - dar]

Beaux yeux, beaux yeux de - puis que je vous ad - mi - re je n'en
[bo zjø bo zjø də - pyi kə ʒə vu zad - mi - rə ʒə nã

suis pas plus heu - reux.
syi pa ply zø - rø]

Fray Fe -li - pe ¿Duer - mes tú?
[fre fe -li - pe dwɛr - mes tu

To - ca la cam - pa - na, Tin - tín, tan
to - ka la kam - pa - na tin tin tan]

Frè - re Jac - ques, dor - mez vous? Son - nez les ma - ti - ne, din, don.
[frɛ -rə ʒa - kə dɔr - me vu sɔ - ne le ma - ti - nə dɛ̃ dɔ̃]

Ha - shi - ve - nu ha - shem e - ley - cha V' - na - shu - va cha - desh
[ha - ʃi - ve- nu ha - ʃem e - lei - xa ve - na - ʃu - va xa - deʃ

ya - me - nu k' - ke - dem.
ja - me - nu ke- ke- dem]

Ha - va na - shi - ra shir ha - le - lu - ja.
[ha - va na - ʃi - ra ʃir ha - le - lu - ja]

He - nay ma tov hu' - ma na - im she - vet a - chim gam ya - chad.
[hi - nei ma tov hu - ma na - im ʃe - vet a - xim gam ja - xad]

Ding, daing, ding, daing, C'est la clo - che du ma - tin, qui
[dɛ̃ dɛ̃ dɛ̃ dɛ̃ se la klɔ - ʃə dy ma - tɛ̃ ki

sonne au le - ver du jour: Bon - jour, bon - jour!
sɔ- no lə - ve dy ʒur bɔ̃ - ʒur bɔ̃ - ʒur]

Lo yis - sa goy el goy che - rev, Lo yil - me - du od mil - cha - mah.
[lo ji - sa goi el goi xe - rev lo jil - me - du od mil - xa - ma]

Mon coq est mort. Il ne di - ra plus co - co - di.
[mɔ̃ kɔ ke mɔr il nə di - ra ply kɔ - kɔ - di]

Sha - lom cha - ve - rim! Le - hit - ra - ot, sha - lom!
[ʃa - lom xa - ve - rim le - hit - ra - ot ʃa - lom]

OTHER USEFUL COLLECTIONS

Bárdos, Lajos. *Hetven Kánon*. Budapest: Zeneműkiadó, 1970.

Cass-Beggs, Rosemary, ed. *The Penguin Book of Rounds*. New York: Penquin Books, 1977.

Fredborg, Klari, and Jørgen Sindberg, eds. *Kanonsang I Skolen*. Egtved: Musikhøjskolens Forlag, 1968.

Hilton, John, ed. *Catch That Catch Can*. New York: Da Capo Press, 1970.

Jöde, Fritz, ed. *Der Kanon*. Wolfenbüttel: Mösler Verlag, 1958.

Langstaff, John, ed. *The Season for Singing*. Garden City: Doubleday and Company, Inc. 1974.

Molnár, Antal, ed. *Klasszikus Kánonok*. Budapest: Zeneműkiadó, 1955.

One Hundred-One Rounds for Singing. World Around Songs, Route 5, Burnsville, NC 28714 USA.

Ravenscroft, Thomas, ed. *Pammelia, Deuteromelia, Melismata, 1609 and 1611*. reprint, Philadelphia: The American Folklore Society, Inc., 1961.

Simpson, Kenneth, ed. *A First Round Book*. Kent: Novello and Company Ltd., 1959.

Simpson, Kenneth, ed. *Seventy-Seven Rounds and Canons*. Kent: Novello and Company Ltd., 1959.

Stainer, John, ed. *The School Round Book*. London: Novello and Company Ltd., 1852.

Taylor, Mary C., ed. *Rounds and Rounds*. New York: William Sloane Associates, 1946.

Walsh, I., ed. *The Catch Club or Merry Companion, 1762*. reprint, Farnborough: Gregg International Publishers Limited, 1965.

ALPHABETICAL INDEX